The Privilege of Prayer

BY
Karen Faith McGowan

II Chronicles 7:14
"If my people, which are called by my name, shall humble themselves, and pray, and seek my face, and turn from their wicked ways; then will I hear from heaven, and will forgive their sin, and will heal their land."

The Privilege of Prayer

ISBN10:   0-9802492-2-8
ISBN13:   978-0-9802492-2-4

For book ordering information or to schedule a speaking engagement, please contact:

Karen Faith McGowan
P.O. Box 204534
Augusta, Georgia 30917-4534
706-449-2863

Email FTF@knology.net or mail to:

Published By:
Christian Writers Network
4104-C Colben Blvd.
Evans, Georgia 30809
(706) 210-1000

Dedication

I dedicate this book to the One who has made it possible for me to understand the importance of prayer and who has taught me how to pray…God's Holy Spirit.

Through meditation on the scriptures and through prayer, God has revealed to me the most sacred aspect of my walk with Him…the privilege of prayer.

Acknowledgment

I would like to thank the women of Faith Baptist Church. In obedience to the urging of the Holy Spirit to deepen my own personal prayer life and in preparation for a presentation to you on this topic, this book came into being. So, in this respect, you are partly responsible for the good that will come from our efforts to help others grow in their relationship with God. Now we all know that this can only be accomplished through our "ACTS" of prayer.

May God bless all those who read these pages and the scriptures contained therein.

Sweet Hour of Prayer

By Karen Faith McGowan · January 2008

Alone in the darkness
Such a peaceful place to be
Words are softly spoken
Between my Lord and me.

He gives me calming reassurance
That He is always there
Sometimes it's in the silence
That He says, "I really do care."

So many problems
To lay at His feet
One by one and in His time
My needs He will surely meet.

Songs of praise
My heart will sing
I am His servant
And He is my King.

When no one else will answer
I know my God always will
His answer may come quickly
But He may say, "Just be still."

Oh the blessing
Of a moment with Him alone
There's peace and contentment
No greater love has ever been known.

He is never too busy
He always has the time
To say, "I will take your burdens,
And I will make them mine."

There's never a heartache
That He cannot bear
If I just take it to Him
In a sweet, sweet hour of prayer.

Table of Contents

Introduction

Prayer...is the most important, yet most neglected activity in the Christian life.

Why is it that we fail to take advantage of our privilege to go to God in prayer? Could it be that we have not yet learned the true meaning of prayer, its purpose, or even how to pray effectively?

In this condensed book on the magnified subject of prayer, we will be discussing these issues, in hopes that together we will develop a greater understanding of how to pray and why prayer is not only necessary, it is essential if we are to have a relationship with God.

"Prayer" - not an obligation, but a privilege

Prayer means: *to connect, communicate, worship, praise, offer thanksgiving, and present our supplications to God.*

In this respect, it is the greatest privilege we have in our spiritual walk with Him. Just to think about being connected with the creator of the universe is overwhelming. It also amazes me that God loves us so much that He wants to include us in His plan for His kingdom. Through the privilege of prayer, we have the opportunity to be a part of His divine purpose.

How is His will interpreted to our hearts? It is through our act of prayer and by the power of the Holy Spirit who connects us heart to heart with God.

The mere whisper of His name gets God's attention. Isaiah 58:9 says, *"Then shalt thou call, and the Lord shall answer; thou shalt cry, and he shall say, Here I am."* He is always one breath away from hearing our petitions.

Prayer is conversation with God. (talking and listening)
Prayer is an earnest plea or supplication.
Prayer is an encounter with God.
Prayer is to contend for our case before our High Priest.
Prayer is essential in order to have a relationship with God.

The scriptures are full of references to Christians seeking God in prayer. The first call upon the New Testament church was to "pray." In Acts 1:14, the church is found continuously seeking the face of God. The verse says, *"These all continued with one accord in prayer and supplication."*

Again in Acts 2:42 we read, *"And they continued steadfastly in the apostles' doctrine and fellowship, and in breaking of bread, and in prayers."*

In Acts chapter three, Peter and John are on their way to what we call today, *"a prayer meeting."*

The disciples, taught by Jesus Christ himself, knew the importance of the connection He had with His Heavenly Father and they desired that same connection for themselves.

Jesus had a thirst for communion with His Father and would often slip away to a quiet place to pray to His Heavenly Father. Many times He would pray for hours. Can you imagine the power God would release if all His children would devote themselves to pray as Jesus did?

The apostle Paul encouraged us to *"pray without ceasing."* This takes specific **"ACTIONS."**

A-dore Him. Our purpose here on earth is that we bring honor and glory to God.

C-onfess our sins. If we confess our sins, He is faithful and just to forgive us our sins and to cleanse us from all unrighteousness.

T-hank Him for all things, by *FAITH* – "For **A**ll **I** **T**hank **H**im"

I-nvest time in meditating on God's word.

O-bey the Holy Spirit and His guidance

N-in the "name of Jesus" make your requests known unto God.

S-ubmission to the will and purpose of God

Many times we redesign prayer in order to fit it in to the busyness of our lives. In doing so, we have forgotten what the heart of prayer really is. It is *"our relationship with God."*

Prayer is to be a time of separation from the world in order to be alone with God. To be separated we must surrender our schedules, our priorities and our lives to receive the joy of spending time alone with Him.

7

In our prayer time, we experience God's love for us and express our love to Him. It's a mutual exchange of talking and listening. It's a time to commit our lives to Jesus Christ and express our will to obey Him. During our prayer time, our souls receive nourishment and strength to be over-comers in this life.

Prayer is the way we communicate our needs, wishes, desires, and even mistakes. It is the way God responds to us. It is our time to gaze into the faces of our Heavenly Father and His Son, Jesus Christ, and to be led by the Holy Spirit in "holy conversation."

Is prayer a priority in your life? Is it the first thing you do when trouble strikes, temptation comes, your needs are overwhelming, or sorrow overshadows your days? Prayer should be our way of life, but many times it becomes our last resort. So often, it consists of our pleas, "gimee, gimee," instead of our praise.

Christianity is not a religion, it is a relationship and a relationship requires communication. Therefore, prayer is essential if we want to communicate with our Heavenly Father. In our lives, there are countless decisions to be made, there is wisdom to be sought, and love, gratitude, and appreciation to be expressed. We achieve these things through prayer.

Surprising as it may seem, the most important aspect of our prayer life is not about petitioning God with our requests, but rather listening to the Holy Spirit. Words uttered in haste are useless unless accompanied by silence as we listen for the Holy Spirit to lead, guide and direct us.

To *"pray without ceasing"* means to be in a constant, never-ending mode of praise, worship, and thanksgiving to God for all things. If we consider our communication with God only as a means of presenting our long list of needs, we miss out on the real purpose of prayer, which is to connect with God.

God calls us to pray and our communication with Him creates intimate fellowship with our Savior. Through prayer we discover God's goodness and faithfulness.

When we develop a prayerful attitude, prayer becomes our first instinct when we encounter a difficulty. We won't even have to think about it. Our attention will just turn immediately and automatically to prayer. In other words, it will never occur to us "NOT" to pray.

God is interested in even the trivial things in our lives. He hears every prayer, even little things like losing our keys. Our needs are important to God and He promises to supply them according to His riches in glory.

But what the Lord really wants to give us, through prayer, is Himself. Only through prayer can we tap into the limitless resources of God. Only by praying can we test the promises of God. John 14:14 says, *"If you shall ask any thing in my name, I will do it."* Prayer is one of the best ways we have to remind ourselves that God is our gracious Heavenly Father and that we are His much loved children and therefore, joint heirs with Christ.

Seeking God in prayer allows us to build a life that has eternal consequences and rewards, as we serve God and others. God is not impressed by lofty or repetitive words with no personal meaning. What God desires is that we communicate with Him in a language that we both understand and that it comes straight from our hearts.

A deeper Christian walk begins with making the decision to spend time alone with God in prayer. All believers should have precious, intimate times with Him. In James 4:8, the Bible tells us to *"Draw nigh to God and He will draw nigh to you."* We are never more than a whisper of a prayer away from our Heavenly Father; through our intercessor, Jesus Christ, and by the power of the Holy Spirit that lives within every believer. How awesome it is to be eternally connected to our Creator, the giver of life, through His Holy Spirit.

Our "Prayer Closet" shouldn't be a place where we just visit when we have a need.
It's where we should live on a constant basis.

The Lord's Prayer - Our Model

The disciples were always in a constant mode of learning from Jesus, so it was comfortable for them to ask Him, "Lord, teach us to pray." In Matthew 6, Jesus teaches the disciples the "model prayer." But first He gave them these instructions:

Verse 5: *"And when thou prayest, thou shalt not be as the hypocrites are, for they love to pray standing in the synagogues and in the corners of the streets, that they may be seen of men."*
Our public prayers are virtually worthless, unless they are accompanied by our private prayers.
Verse 6: *"But thou, when thou prayest, enter into thy closet, and when thou hast shut thy door, pray to thy Father which is in secret."*

9

Verse 7: *"But when ye pray, use not vain repetitions, as the heathen do, for they think that they shall be heard for their much speaking"* God is not impressed with well articulated, pious, prayers from our mouths. His desire is for a sincere and grateful prayer from our hearts.

Verse 8: *"Be not ye therefore like unto them: for your Father knoweth what things ye have need of, before ye ask him."*

Verse 9: Then Jesus said, *"After this manner therefore pray ye."* Jesus gave the disciples and generations to come, a "pattern for prayer." It is displayed for us in what has come to be known as "The Lord's Prayer." (Matthew 6:9-13)

P - *(Praise)* *"Our Father which art in heaven, Hallowed be Thy name."* Jesus introduced a radically new idea by addressing God as **Father**. The word Jesus spoke is represented in English as "Abba," which is similar to our word Dad. This particular address separates Christianity from other religions because it shows that people can have a personal relationship with God, as our Heavenly Father. The word **hallowed** means *"honored as holy."*

R - *(Respect)* *"Thy kingdom come. Thy will be done in earth, as it is in heaven."* **Thy kingdom come** is not just a reference of Christ's second coming, but it also expresses a desire for God to rule in our lives and that God's will to be done – today – **in earth as it is in heaven**.

A - *(Ask)* *"Give us this day our daily bread.* Jesus taught us to pray for **our daily bread**, trusting Him for providing our every need. *And forgive us our debts, as we forgive our debtors."* This is a request for **forgiveness of sin** that we may **forgive** others.

Y - *(Yield)* *"And lead us not into* **temptation**. James 1:13 says that God does not tempt anyone. Our prayer is that He would help us not to fall into temptation. We have the responsibility to run from temptation, (I Corinthians 10:13) but we must also understand the warfare that exists in the spiritual realm.

E - *(Expect)* *"but deliver us from evil:"* God has the power to **deliver us from evil**.

10

𝓡 - (𝓡eward) "*For thine is the kingdom, and the power, and the glory, forever, Amen*". A promise of eternal life in heaven exists for those who believe. God reigns supreme, He is all powerful, and He demands that He be glorified.

"𝒜cts" of 𝒫rayer

It is not unusual for us to be unsure of how to pray. Sometimes, even a seasoned Christian has difficulty in knowing how to approach God in prayer.

In order for our prayer life to be effective, purposeful, and successful, we must be willing to perform what I like to call, the "ACTS" of prayer. James 5:16 says, "*the effectual, fervent prayer of a righteous man availeth much.*" As Christians, we want to feel that our prayers are effective and we long to see the results.

We have discussed the model prayer and actions that we should take. I believe that Jesus was also delivering to the disciples a method to their prayers. In order to simplify and remove the fear of not knowing how to pray, I would like for us to take the "acts" out of "actions." I believe these acts, when performed, will guide us into a more fulfilling, purposeful, and productive prayer life.

Keep in mind that the purpose of our prayers is not that we get what we want, but that God gets what He wants.

𝒜

𝒜doration

𝒞

𝒞onfession

𝒯

𝒯hanksgiving

𝒮

𝒮upplication

𝒜doration - God's will in every circumstance in our life, is that we adore, honor, and glorify Him. Why do you think this is so?

It is because adoring Him is the most direct means by which we can declare our dependence on God. It shows Him that we trust Him,

11

even in the darkness. It confesses our allegiance and devotion to the One who was crucified for us and to whom we are eternally joined.

Peter and John obviously learned their lesson well. In Acts we read of their allegiance to Almighty God as they began their prayer, *"Lord, thou art God, which hast made heaven, and earth, and the sea and all that in there is."*

We are the ones who benefit from adoring God. Why?

- **Adoration magnifies God**. It puts our focus on Him, not our problems. Praising God transforms our thinking as we focus on His power, presence and ability.
- **Adoration humbles us**. When we worship God, we gain a right view of ourselves. Praising Him deflates our ego and eliminates our pride, which strengthens us against temptation.
- **Adoration reveals our devotion to God**. If we adore Him, we are giving Him first place in our lives.
- **Adoration motivates us to holy living**. It opens our hearts to the desire to live the way God desires – holy and separated unto Him. Our desire is to do His will above our own. The more we adore Him, the more we will want to be like Him.
- **Adoration increases our joy**. Joy is the constant companion of adoration. Praising God will eliminate our depression, discouragement, and disappointments.
- **Adoration establishes our faith**. The greater we see God, the smaller we see ourselves and our problems.
- **Adoration elevates our emotions**. Worry, fear, doubt, and confusion cannot exist for long in an atmosphere of praise.

*When we adore Him, we **"worship"** Him*

To worship means *"to awaken the conscience of our hearts to the holiness of God."* In Matthew 22:37, we are called to *"love the Lord thy God with all thy heart, and with all thy soul, and with all thy mind."* When we pray, we open our hearts to His love, we feed our minds on His truth, and we devote our will to His purpose. It is then that we can achieve true worship.

There is no set way to worship the Lord. Some may sense a need to lift their hands in praise, while others may sit with their head bowed, eyes closed, softly uttering words of praise. No matter how we worship, if it is not done with a prayerful heart, it amounts to nothing but hypocrisy before God. As we bow before Him, let it be in a spirit of dependence, humility, and recognition of our frailty without Him.

Worshipping our Lord in prayer is all about Him and not us. When we pray, we sense a lifting of negative circumstances and our focus allows us to view them through His eyes.

Whether in corporate worship or in a time of personal adoration, our prayers will be acceptable to God when He has guided us to worship Him.

*When we adore Him, we **"praise"** Him*

Many of us think of praising God only when things are going great or in times of blessings. We must realize that God is worthy of our praise, even in the bad times. In actuality, *we will never know the power of praise, until we learn its value in our trials.*

Let's discuss some benefits of praising God:

Our praise:

- Puts our attention on God, not on our problem.
- Causes us to recognize that God is sovereign. He knows all things and has a reason and purpose for allowing all things.
- Calls to our remembrance mighty acts of God and answered prayers in our past.
- Prepares our hearts to receive God's awesome power in our lives.
- Helps us to see God as He is - all powerful.
- Makes His presence more real to us.
- Increases our faith.
- Opens our eyes to God's will for our lives.
- Exalts His name.
- Unites the hearts of God's people.
- Fills our hearts with joy and the peace of God.

When it seems our burdens are too heavy to bear, we have a choice. We can fall into depths of despair and make Satan happy or we can rejoice in the sovereign will of Almighty God. We can point fingers, blame others, and be angry at God, or we can praise Him. Why? Because, He is the only true, living God who is capable of turning our sorrows into joy; even our most difficult trials.

Finding it hard to rejoice today? Praise God for "all" things: past, present, and future. Thank Him for loving you enough to teach you, through your trials, the lessons you would never learn otherwise.

Confession

Probably one of the most quoted verses on confession of sins is Romans 10:9-10 which says, "...*that if thou shalt confess with thy mouth the Lord Jesus, and shalt believe in thine heart that God hath raised Him from the dead, thou shalt be saved. For with the heart man believeth unto righteousness; and with the mouth confession is made unto salvation."*

In I John 1:9 we read, "*If we confess our sins, he is faithful and just to forgive us our sins, and to cleanse us from all unrighteousness."*

The psalmist wrote, "*If I regard iniquity in my heart, the Lord will not hear me."*

These verses are speaking to the lost and giving direction for a way to salvation. But confession of sins is not a one time occurrence in our lives. Every day we must die to self and every moment we must live in an attitude of repentance of sins. Prayer allows us the opportunity to respond to the Holy Spirit at the moment of committing sin, so that repentance is given, confession is made, and forgiveness received. Remaining in this attitude allows us to live in fellowship with God because the one thing that separates us from fellowship with Him is our sins.

Repentance means that we take responsibility for our act(s) of sin. When we sin, it is the Holy Spirit who convicts our hearts and gives us opportunity to repent. But it is our choice to listen and obey His prompting.

Matthew 3:2 says, "*Repent ye: for the kingdom of heaven is at hand."* Realizing our sinfulness, repenting of our sins, and accepting God's forgiveness at the point of our salvation is, of course, the most important decision we will ever make. That is because God calls sinners to repentance. In Mark 2:17 Jesus says, "*I came not to call the righteous, but sinners to repentance."*

So, what is it that leads us to repentance? It is the goodness of God. In Romans 2:4 we read of the expression of God's love as His grace towards us, "...*the goodness of God leadeth thee to repentance."* God's grace is unmerited and undeserved, but freely given.

I Timothy 6:12 says that we should "*fight the good fight of faith, lay hold on eternal life, whereunto thou art also called, and hast professed a good profession before many witnesses.*" In other words, God expects us to make our confession public and to be bold in doing so. He says that if we will confess Him before men, He will intercede on our behalf before our Heavenly Father.

Hebrews 3:1 refers to Christ as the High Priest of our profession, "...who *was faithful to Him who appointed him.*" What a privilege it is to be able to approach the throne of God through our High Priest, Jesus Christ. What an honor it is to be able to confess our sins and receive forgiveness. How awesome it is to have Him representing us before Almighty God, the ruler of the universe!

In Hebrews 4:14-16 we read, *"Seeing then that we have a great high priest, that is passed into the heavens, Jesus the Son of God, let us hold fast our profession. For we have not an high priest which cannot be touched with the feelings of our infirmities; but was in all points tempted like as we are, yet without sin. Let us therefore come boldly unto the throne of grace, that we may obtain mercy, and find grace to help in time of need."*

To walk in the spirit of confession of sins is to walk in fellowship with the Holy Spirit and in righteousness with God, through our Lord Jesus. Un-confessed sin does not break our "union" with God, but it does break our "communion" with Him.

Thanksgiving

I Thessalonians 5:18 says, *"In everything give thanks; for this is the will of God in Christ Jesus concerning you."* This means even when we may not understand what God is doing and life is a struggle. Colossians 4:2 says, *"Continue in prayer, and watch in the same with thanksgiving."*

How many times do we tell God how much we appreciate Him? How often do we tell Him how thankful we are for what His Son did for us at Calvary? Do we tell Him enough how grateful we are that He provided a way for us to have eternal life in heaven with Him?

In order to understand the importance of always being grateful, regardless of the circumstances, we must know the answers to two questions:

Why are we to give thanks in everything?
How are we to do so?

Why are we to give thanks in everything?

We express our thanks to God not always because we always feel grateful, but because it is His command.

Expressing gratitude with a thankful heart:
- keeps us continually aware of His presence
- means we are talking to Him
- motivates us to look for His purpose
- helps us to be aware of our dependence on God
- builds our faith and trust in Him
- makes us mindful of His presence
- has a powerful impact on those who are witnessing our thankfulness, especially when we are going through trials.
- gives us opportunity to share that God gives us strength, moment by moment, to enable us to press through our difficulties.

How are we to do so?

The Holy Spirit gives Christians the strength for impossible tasks, even praising God for our trials and tribulations. It is a privilege that only those of us who know Him can have. Even if we don't have one single, logical reason to thank Him, the Holy Spirit will enable us to have the power to express our gratitude and thanksgiving.

Let us be thankful as the apostle Paul, who found himself to be content, even while chained in prison. Or Job, who lost everything, yet continued to trust God and be thankful for his relationship with Him. Or David, a man after God's own heart, who sinned against God, yet repented and subsequently recorded the beautiful psalms in honor of a holy God; the One he trusted and had faith in to forgive him and deliver him from his enemies.

When we can understand the why and the how, we can have victory in every situation and it will be so worth the battle as we walk in the power of a prayerful and thankful heart.

List some things that you are thankful for? Now take a look at your list. Does it include the things that are hard to be thankful for? In your prayer time, have you stopped to thank God for your difficulties, trials, disappointments, and challenges? The scriptures tell us to give thanks in "all" things. So this means not only during times of blessing, but also during the most difficult times in our lives. It is during these times that we will grow the most if we will fervently seek God in prayer.

When we allow God to use our circumstances to mold us, teach us, refine us, and purify us, we are giving Him permission to make us more like Christ. Spiritual growth is evident when we can see past the problem to the process; and through the provision to the purpose. The more we yield to the working of the Holy Spirit in our lives, the more we are able to humble ourselves before Him. It is then that we can put emphasis on what has eternal significance which is *"glorifying God."*

Supplication

The word supplication means to **beg, plead, or make our needs known.** Our cry of humility conveys to God our total helplessness and dependence on Him to supply all our needs according to His riches in glory, through Christ Jesus.

After we have spent time in adoration, confession, and thanksgiving, it is amazing how insignificant the supplication of our needs sometimes becomes. Yet, God wants us to name our needs one by one and He wants us to be specific.

Though He is already aware of our every need:
- It is, most of the time, the very thing that brings us into His presence.
- It is our needs that humble us as we see our frailty and weakness compared to God and His strength, especially when we are facing a difficult decision.
- It is our needs that force us to take a look at our priorities and evaluate whether what we think is a need - is really a desire.
- It is our need that forces us to be dependent on God for the answer.
- It is also our desire to have our needs fulfilled that forces us to listen for God's answer.

God also desires that we be persistent in our prayer life. Many times we stop praying for a particular request when we fail to see results. God uses our persistence and determination as a measure of our faith and trust in Him to provide an answer: in His time, His way, and according to His plan. As children of God, we must pray and expect God to answer in this way.

Presenting our needs to God requires a heart that is submitted to His will and obedient to His provision, which may be totally opposite of what we asked for. God knows what is best for us and He will always give us what we need. He will also take away the things that He knows will hinder our relationship with Him: things such as wealth, position, fame or even relationships.

Are you willing to present your supplications to God with a humble, obedient heart that is ready to accept His best for you?

Before presenting our supplications to God, we should always ask ourselves:

- Would my request honor God?
- Would my request advance His kingdom?
- Would my request help others?
- Would it help me to grow spiritually?

We all want our prayers to be effective, so the next time you pray, remember the four *"ACTS"* of prayer:

:

Adoration (praise and worship Him)
Confession (repent *of any known sin*)
Thanksgiving (for "all" things), then
Supplication (make our requests known unto God)

We pray:

"To"– our Heavenly Father – who reigns
"In "– the name of His Son, Jesus Christ – who intercedes
"By"– the power of the Holy Spirit – who enables

When we pray in this way, God will hear our prayers and
He will answer.

The Price of Prayerlessness

Let's imagine you decided to move from your current residence to a home across town. You've never been there before, so you have no idea what to expect. You don't know the people who will be your new neighbors and you are unaware of how much work your new place will need.

Friends come by to offer you help with packing, but you decline by saying, "I can do it by myself." You struggle with lifting heavy boxes and, at times, they seem almost too burdensome to carry.

You finally get the rental truck loaded with your personal belongings, when another friend drops by to offer his assistance driving the truck. Again, you refuse saying, "I can do it by myself." Since you have never been to your new home, you get lost. It takes you much longer to find your way because, though you were offered directions, you said, "I can find the way by myself."

When you finally arrive, you find that your new home is in much need of repair. Your new neighbors, realizing that you are all alone, offer to help you make your new place livable. Again you say, "I can do it by myself."

Eventually, you find yourself sitting in the middle of a dark, lonely, run down room and wonder how in the world you are going to "do it all by yourself." Your body is aching from pulling and lifting. You are hungry, cold, and so physically exhausted that you don't see how you could possibly face another day like this. The burden of it all is overwhelming and thus you start to say, "I can't do this by myself anymore!"

Before you could complete the sentence, you hear a voice saying, *"I've been waiting for you to ask for my help. I've been here all along. I wanted to help you carry the burden and the heavy load. I also wanted to have your new home prepared for your arrival, but you kept refusing my help, sent by way of your friends, family, and neighbors. You failed to ask for my assistance until you had exhausted all your energy trying to do it all on your own. I am here now. Cast your burden upon Me, for I care for you and I will help you. I will repair the windows, re-do the floors, and put a new coat of paint on the walls. Before long your home will look like a new one and within its walls will abide the spirit of God."*

Our Heavenly Father has called us to lay our burdens at His feet. When we fail to come to Him in prayer, we are just as foolish as the person who refused help with the move; always mumbling and thinking, "I can do it by myself." The truth is, we "can't" do it by ourselves and God never intended for us to try. The whole time we are struggling with doing things our way and in our own strength, we are missing out on fellowship with God and the blessings and rewards that come from doing so.

Jesus never fails. His mercy is new every morning. Philippians 4:6 says, *"Let your requests be made known unto God."* Prayer is the one thing that changes the direction of our thoughts and our activity and this is guided by our heart. Prayer puts our focus on God and not on ourselves and our capabilities. Are you willing to pay the price of prayerlessness?

Praying in the "Name of Jesus"

There is power in the name of Jesus and we are clearly instructed to use His name in our prayers. It is often used to close the prayers of the faithful and obedient, when it should be one of the first words out of our mouths.

As Jesus prepared to depart from this earth, He gave this instruction: *"And whatever ye shall ask in my name, that will I do, that the Father may be glorified in the Son. If ye shall ask anything in my name, I will do it."* (John 14:13-14)

However, we must be careful not to misinterpret what Jesus was saying. Simply tacking on His name at the end of our prayers does not automatically guarantee results. There are three very important parts that we must include:

- *Our hearts must be devoted to glorifying Him in all that we say or do.*
- *We need to always ask according to the will of our Heavenly Father.*
- *We must also agree with God's purpose.*

Presenting our supplications in the name of Jesus declares our "Association with the Savior." The one thing that makes it possible for us to approach God in prayer is our relationship with Jesus. The presence of Christ living within us proves that we are one of His own; purchased by His blood and joint heirs with Him, as children adopted into the family of God.

Presenting our supplication in the name of Jesus also guarantees our "Access to the Father." Christ's death prepared the way for us to have unhindered admittance to the Father's presence. When He died on the cross, the veil in the temple, which had separated God from man, was rent in two. This provides for us today a symbolism that access to God is now available to all who will just believe.

Therefore, praying in the name of Jesus states our relationship with Christ and our right, through Him, to approach our Heavenly Father. It gives us authority to petition God, through Christ who sits at His right hand to intercede on our behalf. Everyone who has received Christ has been granted the privilege to use His name when petitioning God.

To use His name, *we must also agree with God's purposes.* It means we are asking in agreement with His character and will. When we allow His word to abide in us, it becomes part of our thinking and standard for life.

"In Jesus' name" evokes confidence in our belief that He hears and answers our prayers.

Praying in Jesus name must *glorify God. It must also be in likeness to the things Jesus Himself would ask.* Always ask yourself: "Is this request, made in the name of Jesus, based on ideals, values, decisions, and principles that Jesus would support?" If not, don't expect Him to acknowledge a request made in His name, when it doesn't align with His character.

Praying the "Bible" Way

No doubt, most of us, as children, were taught to recite one or more "children's prayers." Even many non-believers are able to recite "Now I lay me down to sleep," or "God is great, God is good."

Learning the concept of communicating with God is vitally important for our children. However, these repetitive prayers lose their value as we mature in our spiritual walk.

Let's look at Matthew 7:7, 8 &11. *"Ask and it shall be given you; seek, and ye shall find; knock, and it shall be opened unto you: For every one that asketh receiveth; and he that seeketh findeth; and to him that knocketh it shall be opened. If ye then, being evil, know how to give good gifts unto your children, how much more shall your Father which is in heaven give good things to them that ask him?"*

What is it that we are to learn from this passage? That God wants us to pursue Him in our prayer life by asking, seeking and knocking; expecting with confidence His answer to meet our needs. Jesus used these three words to help us pray effectively.

"Ask" – By coming to God with our requests, we are acknowledging our need and our belief in God's ability to meet it.

21

"Seek" – God wants us to get involved in the situation we are praying about. It is one thing to seek His wisdom, but it is another to put that wisdom into action, while taking steps towards finding God's answer to our need. He doesn't expect us to just sit idly by, waiting for Him to reveal His answer and solve all our problems. When we are walking with the Holy Spirit in obedience, God will provide the answer. Our job is to keep walking.

"Knock" – There is no doubt that we are going to meet obstacles along the way. By staying in consistent and sustained prayer, we are exhibiting our will to seek God's answer and this will also open our eyes to the open door that we should enter with confidence because it will always be a provision of God. Prayer is such a privilege and a key component in the Christian life. It opens the door for us to not only approach God, but to also involve Him in our lives.

These three words: "ask, seek, and knock," are "active verbs." This means that they require active participation in the process. Our Heavenly Father wants us to pursue Him with all our hearts. He wants to be known by all His children. To seek Him, we must seek His presence, His wisdom, His character, and His will for our lives.

In Jeremiah 33:3, God told Jeremiah, *"Call unto me and I will answer thee, and show thee great and mighty things, which thou knowest not."* God is interested in every detail of our lives and He wants to hear from us.

Asking God helps us to distinguish between our real needs and what we may perceive as a need. If God were to give us everything thing we wanted, we would, more than likely, drift in our devotion and prayer life with Him.

It is a good thing to pray and ask God to show you exactly where you might be missing His best. If you have erected walls between you and God's blessing, these will have to come down. Trust Him. Let Him know that you are willing to allow Him to meet the needs of your life.

Praying to God doesn't mean reciting repetitive words to some distant deity. We need to be intimate with God. He knows all about us anyway. He wants to know how much we are willing to expose our innermost thoughts and feelings to Him.

In return, His Holy Spirit will enlighten us, giving us wisdom and understanding. Our prayer time with God should be the most precious part of our day, because we will be spending consistent, quality time with our most respected, loyal, and faithful friend. Prayer should be a natural expression of our feelings, concerns, thoughts and emotions

22

throughout our entire day and they should be directed to the One who cares most about every aspect of our lives, Jesus Christ.

The Bible also tells us to pray without doubting. In James 1:2-8, we are encouraged to pray whole-heartedly unto the Lord as verse 8 says, *"A double minded man is unstable in all his ways."* This doesn't mean that if we pray without doubting we will get exactly what we ask for. The key is undivided "trust."

As we grow in our prayer life, we should seek to pray with fervency, zeal, passion, gratefulness, and humility. We should pray "actively" from our hearts; not passively from our childhood memories.

God always answers the prayers of His children, but on His timetable, for His purpose, and for our good. (II Chronicles 6:4) Before you pray, ask yourself if you truly, genuinely trust God for His answer, while you: Ask, Seek, and Knock.

God uses the willing, prayerful hearts of mankind to achieve His purposes

To rescue humanity in the flood – God used Noah.
For the creation of a nation – God used Abraham.
To lead the nation of Israel out of bondage – God used Moses.
To bring the nation of Israel from captivity – God used Joshua.
To bring salvation to the world – God became a man.

Paul - A Man of Prayer

If you went to a bookstore today, no doubt you would be able to find all sorts of "how to" books on anything from home repairs to starting a business, how to lose weight fast, or how to prepare a gourmet meal. But what if you want to improve your prayer life? What book would you choose? One internet site boasts over 8,000 books on the subject of prayer alone.

There is no better choice of books on how to improve your prayer life than God's word. Try studying Bible heroes and the way they prayed. We are going to take a look at one of my favorites, the apostle Paul.

The apostle Paul gives us two examples of how we are to pray. In Colossians 1:9-10, he asks that the people of Colossae may be *"filled with the knowledge of His will in all wisdom and spiritual understanding.*" Here he was teaching the saints that they were to pray according to God's will and not their own desires.

He also asks that they will have more than just an understanding of what is right; he prays, *"that they may walk worthy of the Lord unto all pleasing, being fruitful in every good work, and increasing in the knowledge of God."*

Why did Paul pray for these saints in this way? Because he knew that the transformation in their lives would be a witness to the power of God working in them. Their changed lives would be the evidence of the Father's ability to forgive sin and enable them to walk before Him in holiness. What a testimony of the grace of God and it is achieved through a pattern of prayer.

Paul's "approach" to prayer:

- Paul knew *who he was praying to.*
- He *knew God's character* – both loving Father and Supreme Authority. Therefore, we learn from Him that we approach the Lord with a posture of submission and reverence. Ephesians 3:14-15 says, *"For this cause I bow my knees unto the Father of our Lord Jesus Christ, Of whom the whole family in heaven and earth is named."*
- Paul knew God as *a loving Father* and he prayed that the people of Ephesus would come to know His unconditional love as well.
- Paul also knew to *acknowledge his gratefulness. "Now unto him that is able to do exceeding abundantly above all that we ask or think, according to the power that worketh in us,"* (Ephesians 3:20)

The" content" of his prayers:

- Paul made his requests specific. He prayed for tangible things that he could measure: like patience, strength, and wisdom.
- Paul wasn't afraid to ask for God-sized things. He knew that nothing was too big or too small for God to be interested in, especially when it concerned His children.
- Paul made sure his prayers were Christ centered. His prayers were never for himself, but rather for others and with a

24

servant's heart. They were always in submission to God's authority and with a humble heart.

- Paul's prayers were related to eternity. His concern was always on God's kingdom being increased.
- Paul's prayers brought glory to God. He praised God most of all for His faithfulness.
- Paul knew that *the most powerful way to evoke change in another person's life was through prayer.* It is God who works behind the scenes to build a person's understanding of their need for change or to impress on him/her to have a change in lifestyle. It is our role to keep praying in a Christ centered manner, while He does His work. Paul understood this fact.

It would benefit us to pattern our prayer life around that of the apostle Paul.

Praying When In Need

Life holds many stressful moments. Many times we lack clarity and direction in how to proceed.

Prayer starts with transitioning from what is happening in our world, to focusing on communing with God and thinking only on Him. When we do so, our problems and cares lose their significance. This helps our minds to clear.

God's desire is not only just to provide our needs, but to build up our confidence and belief in Him. (Psalm 46:10) Our faith increases when we see a direct correlation between our requests and His answers. Making a prayer list is a good idea because we can look back over our list to see how God has answered our prayers. It is a good picture of God at work and it builds our faith and belief in the power of prayer.

God knows that one of our greatest needs is that of having wisdom. A request for it is never denied. He never turns us away or criticizes us for asking for more. God's desire is that we have the mind of Christ. *"But he that is spiritual judgeth all things, yet he himself is judged of no man. For who hath known the mind of the Lord, that he may instruct him? But we have the mind of Christ."(* I Corinthians 2: 15-16)

Hindrances to Our Prayers

There are many hindrances that can block the effectiveness of our prayers.

- Not knowing God's will for our situation. God's answer is "yes" when our petition is in agreement with His will and purpose for our lives, but we sometimes forget that "no" is also an answer.
- Having a low expectation that God will answer.
- Doubt can short-circuit our faith and the power of our prayers.
- Sometimes we listen to the wrong voices or base our beliefs on things outside of God's word.
- More commonly, we look at the problem instead of the Provider.
- Sometimes God delays His answer or responds in a way contrary to what we expect. We must be willing to look beyond the problem to the purpose.
- Sin and/or disobedience
- Selfish motives
- Pride
- Unforgiveness – *"And when ye stand praying, forgive, if ye have aught against any; that your Father also which is in heaven may forgive you your trespasses."* (Mark 11:25-26)
- Misplaced priorities

Fasting and Prayer

When Jesus referred to fasting and praying, He was offering His invitation to a deeper experience with God. By placing our physical desires under the Spirit's control, we are able to do without what doesn't matter in order to take hold of what does matter. There are several reasons for fasting.

To cleanse from sin. Fasting in prayer allows us to turn our focus from our rights to "dying to self." It teaches us to sacrifice instead of being self-sufficient. It is easy for unhealthy attitudes to take up residence when there are lapses in our prayer and fasting. We may not notice the change, but God does. His desire is fellowship.

Having our focus in the wrong place not only hinders our fellowship with Him, but also limits the effectiveness of our service. It also displaces our joy. Prayer combined with fasting gives God our undivided attention so that He is able to expose and address areas of sin in our lives.

Guidance. God sometimes requires a cleansed and cleared mind in order for us to hear what He is saying. A submitted spirit is also more ready to accept His instructions.

Protection. Through fasting we gain wisdom and insight into God's ways and the Holy Spirit will give us help in identifying dangerous situations. By submitting to His authority and asking Him, we receive not only His protection, but also discernment to make wiser decisions.

Spiritual awareness. Fasting along with prayer brings a heightened sense of spiritual awareness, by bringing us into a closer connection with God. This should be the deepest desire of our heart and it is so worth the price of fasting.

There is "Power" in Prayer

As Christians, we are a new creation in Christ. Because of this, we can draw strength from God's divine nature that lives within us.

II Peter 1:4 says, *"Whereby are given unto us exceeding great and precious promises: that by these ye might be partakers of the divine nature."*

James 5:16 says, *"The effectual fervent prayer of a righteous man availeth much."* Think of a runner nearing the end of a race. This is his moment of intensity and determination. He releases all his power in attempts to finish the race in first place.

This is the same kind of passion that God wants us to have in our prayer life. We use repetitive phrases such as, "according to Your will," or "in Jesus name," thinking that our petition will surely impress God and bring about His answer. But power is not found in our words, because the Lord cannot be forced to do anything outside of His perfect will. *The power of our prayer life is in God's reaction.* He responds to the prayers of the righteous by releasing His supernatural power toward the object of concern.

There is power in prayer and therefore a *prayer-less person is a power-less person.* God's power is released in accordance with our fervent, continuous, zealous desire for His intervention on our behalf or on the behalf of another person.

A person of fervent prayer will stay on his knees until he has prayed through every barrier that Satan erects. When does he stop? When God answers or when He makes it clear that our request is not in His will. How wonderful it is that we are able to tap into God's supernatural power through prayer.

The power of the Holy Spirit is the strength by which we are enabled to serve God. He dwells within each believer, but that doesn't mean He automatically releases His power in our lives. However, His power is available to every person who is willing to serve Him and meet the following requirements:

First, we must be *convicted of our inadequacies.* There are reasons we must ask God to help us rely on His sufficiency:

Our inadequacies:

- Drive us to God.
- Eliminate the burden of feeling like we have to do things in our own strength.
- Force us to live our lives through the power of the Holy Spirit, not our own.
- Give God the opportunity to show what great things He can do with so little.
- Allow God to use us to our full potential.
- Allow God to receive all the glory.
- Allow us to walk in peace, contentment and quietness of spirit.

Secondly, we must *live a pure life.* Confession of sin and repentance are necessary in order to maintain fellowship with God.

Thirdly, in order to appropriate God's divine energy we must *have an active prayer life.* It is in our daily, consistent conversation with God that we receive the direction of His will for our lives and the power to achieve it.

A Healthy Prayer Life Means "We Are Never Too Busy"

Have you ever neglected your daily prayer time because you felt you were too busy? Whenever we replace our time with God with the

28

busyness of life, we are telling God that He is not our number one priority.

We have all been guilty of this from time to time. We let our schedules determine when, where, and how we will spend time with God. Since we know God is always there, it is easy to assume that we can catch up with Him at a later time, therefore taking His eternal presence in our lives for granted.

Many times, what we fail to realize is that it is during our quiet moments with the Lord that He empowers us to face the many obstacles and challenges of the day. Starting our day in God's presence tells Satan where he stands on our list of important things to do. Walking closely with our Lord also helps us to resist the temptation to sin. In all actuality, the busier our day is expected to be, the more time we should spend in prayer and preparation.

The scriptures clearly show that Jesus was very protective of the time He had with His Heavenly Father. I can't imagine anything we could ever have to do that would have more importance than redeeming the souls of man. Yet, when the burden of sin was greatest upon Him, what did Christ do? He slipped away to pray to His Father.

When your schedule is full, what is the first thing you cut? Protect your time with God and make it your first priority. Jesus is God. If He considered prayer a necessity when preparing for His busiest days, then it should be just as important to the rest of us.

Boldly Approaching God's Throne

God's word tells us to come boldly before God's throne of grace in order to receive mercy and find grace for our every need.

II Corinthians 9:8 says, *"And God is able to make all grace abound toward you; that ye, always having all sufficiency in all things, may abound to every good work."* Our Lord delights in our willingness to approach Him.

*"**Grace**"* is receiving God's unmerited favor. Another way of putting it would be: receiving the things we "don't" deserve, like God's blessings and help. We can be confident to approach His throne in prayer, even though we do not deserve it and in spite of what we do deserve.

*"**Mercy**,"* on the other hand, is God's way of preventing us from receiving what we "do" deserve. His merciful response to our request

and our needs may not always be what we expect, but it will always be in our best interest and for our good.

Many times, I think that we, as Christians, hesitate to approach God's throne for fear of condemnation or judgment. On the contrary, His throne of grace is a place of power, authority, glory, and majesty. It's a place where God the Father resides and rules. It is a place of overflowing, unconditional love, mercy, and goodness and it is available to all those who will come into His presence.

Sitting at the right hand of God is His Son, Jesus Christ, our "High Priest." His blood, which is the sacrifice He paid for our sins, gives us access to our Heavenly Father. Jesus is also our "Intercessor." Christ Jesus, who died, conquered death and rose to new life, defends us before God by offering words of grace, forgiveness, and restoration. The One who is perfect pleads with the Father on our behalf, because of all our imperfections. Oh, what love is this!

There is nothing hidden from the Lord. He knows everything about us and what lies within our hearts. He is able to sympathize with us because He experienced what it was like to be human. He was tempted just as we are.

Because of God's provision of His precious Son, Jesus Christ, we are able to walk daily, continuously, confidently, and boldly before God's throne of grace.

Our Number One Priority

One day, as Jesus was heading to Jerusalem, He stopped at Bethany to visit with His friends Mary, Martha, and their brother, Lazarus. As was customary in those days, Martha was rushing around preparing a meal while Mary sat at the feet of Jesus: attentive to His every word.

Martha fretted, while Mary worshipped her Lord. Mary was a woman who cared more for Jesus and what He had to say than she did doing what was culturally appropriate. Jesus took up for her as He taught Martha this valuable lesson: *our number one priority is to spend time with Him.*

The same is true for us today. Many people think they are proving their love to God by doing things for Him such as: going to church, tithing, or even sharing the Gospel. These things are important, but in themselves, they are empty. Our priority should be to connect with God personally on a regular basis and to spend time with the One who loves us most.

Many times we put off prayer time, saying we are too busy. In all actuality, we would find more hours to accomplish the things we need to do, if we took the time to start our day in the presence of God.

Like Martha, if we neglect to make prayer our priority, we tend to find that one duty leads to another, and another, and then another. By the end of the day, we find ourselves exhausted from trying to accomplish tasks that many times were meaningless, when the most valuable time spent in our day is always with God.

Nothing in life equals what God allows us to have with Him, if we will just make Him our number one priority. God created us with a desire to know Him so that He could make Himself known to us. He never meant for our relationship with Him to be cold, distant, and unreachable. His desire is intimacy with His children. We are His number one priority.

Waiting on God

Psalm 37:7-8 admonishes, *"Rest in the Lord and wait patiently for him:"* Waiting on the Lord means pausing until we receive further instructions on how to proceed, but it doesn't mean to stop what we are doing until we receive those instructions. *It is a purposeful, determined, deliberate, active anticipation of what God is going to do.* Waiting does not mean doing nothing. It is "a firm resolve to trust God until we hear Him tell us exactly what is to be His will." We know that His thoughts are not our thoughts, (Isaiah 55:8) but that His desire for us is always His best.

There are reasons why we should always wait on God's perfect timing:

- *First*, there are numerous accounts in the Bible that indicate God's willingness to give *clear guidance only when we are willing to wait* on it. For example: Noah, Moses, Abraham.
- A *second* reason for God's delay can be that *our decision may affect other people.* While we are waiting, God is arranging all the specifics for the sake of all who may be involved.
- A *third* reason is that *God has to prepare us for the answer.* I Peter 5:6 says that we are to humble ourselves before God so that He may exalt us "in due time."

- *Lastly, God uses a waiting time to get our attention.* He will wait as long as is necessary for us to turn our attention back to Him.

So, what do we do while we are waiting?

- We should turn our attention to meditating on His word.
- We should be careful not to develop an attitude of anger or impatience.
- We should cultivate our listening skills.
- We should maintain our faith and trust in God.
- We should continue in our present circumstances until we receive further instructions.
- We should stay close to Him so that we are able to hear His voice.

On the other hand, what happens if we don't wait?

- If we act before receiving a confirmation from God, we are living in *disobedience.*
- We will *delay God's blessing.* We could even *bring pain and suffering* on ourselves or on those we love.

When thinking about waiting on God, I am again reminded of the story of Mary and Martha. Their brother Lazarus, whom Jesus loved, lay ill and dying. They knew that Jesus had the power to heal him, so they sent word to Jesus of Lazarus's impending death.

His words were, *"This sickness is not unto death, but for the glory of God, that the Son of God might be glorified through it." (John 11:4)*

Have you ever felt like God was not hearing your prayers? Have you ever wondered why He was seemingly withholding His answer? Did you ever wonder why He didn't seem to show up or when He did, if He would be too late?

If our request is out of His will – God says, "NO."
If it's not according to His time – God says, "SLOW."
If our motive is wrong – God says, "GROW."
But, if our request, the time, and our motive is right – God says, "GO!"

I am sure these thoughts must have plagued the minds of Mary and Martha as they awaited the coming of Christ. Four days after the death of Lazarus, Jesus arrived. The sisters didn't understand why He had not come earlier. Though it seemed to them that He was too late, He was right on-time for "His purpose," which was to bring glory to God through Himself.

The power of God was revealed as Jesus gave evidence to His own resurrection, by the resurrecting of his friend, Lazarus. Christ had a lesson to teach the crowd that day and His glory was made known as He said, *"Lazarus, come forth."* Our Lord knew that healing the sick was not nearly as dramatic as raising the dead. He wanted the people to believe that He was the Son of God so badly, that He was willing to wait, in order to be right on time.

Like Mary and Martha, there will be times in our lives, as Christians, that it may seem like God is withholding His answer to our prayers. God's delay may be to insure that the outcome will bring honor and glory to His name.

If our prayers are not according to His will, "no" may be His answer or His silence may mean that He is waiting for us to turn to Him for the grace to accept His will.

A "no" answer doesn't necessarily mean "never." God's timing is not our timing. His answer will come if we continually submit ourselves to Him in prayer; requesting the enlightenment of our hearts to His purpose and the acceptance of His will.

If we become impatient and move ahead of God, we may receive what is good, but we will miss God's best. The more we are communicating with Him in prayer, the more aware we are of the nudging of the Holy Spirit as to what we are supposed to do in every situation in our lives.

As we waiver with decisions, sometimes God allows us to be disappointed in order to steer us towards something more amazing than we could ever have imagined; something that will definitely bring more honor and glory to His name. We might not understand at first, but if we continue to wait, He will bless our faithfulness.

When we take the time to seek God's will in prayer, we must also be willing to take the time to listen for His answer. In the hectic world we live in, nothing is more important than hearing what God has to say to us.

In order to be more willing to wait we must:

Have faith. Meditate on scripture and ask the Holy Spirit to make clear to you the things that seem less obvious.

Seek to have a humble heart. We must realize that we can do nothing apart from Jesus Christ. We must be willing to endure until God sends His answer to our prayer.

Be patient. Waiting patiently is characterized by an inner peace. Philippians 4:7 says, *"And the peace of God, which passeth all undersatanding, shall keep your hearts and minds through Christ Jesus."* Peace comes from believing that God is who He says He is and that He will do as He has promised. Making quick decisions often means making wrong decisions.

Have courage. Courage is not the absence of fear. It is trusting God and doing what He asks us to do, despite the fear. In other words, courage is "faith in action." Even if others disapprove of your decision to wait on the Lord, be continual in your prayers and the Holy Spirit will enable you to stand firm until you are sure of God's answer.

Wait quietly. It will be difficult to hear God's still small voice if we are not waiting in silence.

Trust God. Doubting God limits what He is trying to do in our lives. His word and His promises are true and He is honored when we live out our faith, trust, and confidence in Him.

Be steadfast. God may use other people or circumstances to lead you, but always measure what you are hearing against God's word, not another person's opinion.

Be willing to suffer for the cause of Christ. Sometimes being willing to wait means: suffering through difficult circumstances. God often strengthens us through trials and increases our faith as He undergirds us with the power to endure.

Persevere. One of the greatest hindrances to our prayer life is our lack of perseverance. We live in a microwave world. We expect immediate results, even from our prayer life. God often requires a test of our patience and our desire to persevere in prayer.

Hebrews 1:1-2 assures us that God still speaks today. His communication with us is always for our benefit. When you hear Him speak, you can rest assured that what He is saying is directed to you and only you.

The psalmist wrote, *"I waited patiently for the Lord, and He inclined to me and heard my cry."* God wants us to wait on "Him," not on what we are waiting on Him to do for us.

In Isaiah 40:31 we are given an amazing promise: *"But they that wait upon the Lord shall renew their strength; they shall mount up with wings as eagles; they shall run, and not be weary; and they shall walk, and not faint."* God is faithful to provide a supply of endless strength to those who are willing to wait upon Him.

Prayer Gives Strength

The apostle Paul knew very well what it meant to be tested, but he was also very knowledgeable about the importance of all his painful experiences. He knew that he would find strength in his time of need, through prayer.

We can learn from Paul, and our own lives, that *great strength follows great weakness.* One of the most important lessons in our Christian life is to learn that in our weakest moments, when we feel the most helpless, God is waiting for us to turn to Him. It is during these times that God is able to do His greatest work in and through us by empowering and strengthening us to go on. When we call out His name in desperation saying, "God, I cannot go on without You," we are immediately given God's best as He equips and enables us not only to suffer, but to endure. The only way to experience God's blessing in this way is to know weakness and the strength that erupts from it when we turn to God in prayer.

While we often pray that God will change our circumstances, He most often uses our circumstances to change us.

The Holy Spirit - Our "Helper"

The moment we accept Christ as our Savior, the Holy Spirit sets up residence in our hearts and seals our relationship with God. *It is He who counsels us and teaches us how to pray.*

He has several roles as our Teacher:

- He illuminates the scriptures so that we can understand
- He provides spiritual gifts
- He connects us with God; sealing our relationship as His children.

- He gives discernment. This is why He is called, "The Spirit of Truth." The Holy Spirit is our direct connection with God's mind and He will willingly reveal our next step to us.
- He is also the transporter of communication between God and man.

Prayer is about intimacy with God. As the Holy Spirit teaches, guides and directs our prayers, He communicates with God, especially when we have difficulty expressing our thoughts and feelings. Romans 8:26 says, *"Likewise the Spirit also helpeth our infirmities: for we know not how to pray for as we ought; but the Spirit itself maketh intercession for us with groanings which cannot be uttered."* The groanings of the Holy Spirit are communicated to God in a special way. This is because God searches the believer's heart, and thereby knows the mind of the Spirit.

Instructions from the Holy Spirit are sent to us directly from God. We can be assured of walking in obedience to God's will when we are obeying the prompting of the Holy Spirit.

Sometimes God communicates to us through the Holy Spirit, an answer of "NO!" When our purpose is God's purpose, we realize that no sometimes "is" His best answer.

The Apostle Paul asked three times for his "thorn in the flesh" to be removed. (II Corinthians 12:8) I am sure that there was some length of time between his requests, yet God waited until Paul had begged three times before He denied his request. God had a reason for His no answer to Paul. God was able to use Paul's weakness to prove His strength. Therefore, God was glorified in Paul's weakness and His purpose was achieved.

There are many times in our lives when we feel that our prayers are going no where, but that is not the time to quit. It's the time to ask for help from the Comforter who lives within us, the Holy Spirit.

God is always listening attentively to our prayers and supplications, but in patience we must pray through these circumstances until God gives an answer. Instead of giving up, ask the Holy Spirit to help you be patient and persevere in prayer, just as Paul did.

As Jesus neared His time of death, He frequently referred to the Helper He would be sending. *One of the Holy Spirit's most significant roles is as our Helper in prayer.* The burden we feel to pray comes from Him. He knows about what lies ahead of us and He knows that we will find the strength and endurance to get through it by drawing closer to the Father. Therefore, He prompts us to talk to Him. The last thing we should do is ignore the prompting of the Holy Spirit to pray. In I Thessalonians 5:19 we are told to *"quench not the Spirit."* In other words, to ignore the prompting of the Holy Spirit is actually a sin.

Through the burden placed upon us by the Holy Spirit to pray, we are experiencing God's love. He uses our prayer life to desensitize us to the battles of life and to turn our focus on Him. Listening and obeying the prompting of the Holy Spirit is our way of showing our love in return.

There are many reasons for weakness in our prayer life. We may have difficulty concentrating or feel unworthy, guilty, or unsure of our faith. Many times our feelings of inadequacy are brought on by the discouragement we may feel, which, by the way, comes straight from the enemy. Whenever we feel resistance in our prayer life, we should ask the Holy Spirit to strengthen, assist, and intercede for us.

Praying for Discernment

King Solomon learned a valuable lesson on prayer in a dream (I Kings 3:5-14) when God said, *"Ask what I shall give thee."* Solomon was humbled by his succession of his father, Kind David, and he knew that he lacked wisdom to rule the people. He said, *"I am but a little child: I know not how to go out or come in."*

But in verse 9, he asked God, *"Give therefore thy servant an understanding heart to judge thy people, that I may discern between good and bad."*

God was pleased with his request for wisdom, rather than long life, riches, or the life of his enemies. God therefore granted him wisdom and discernment, as well as riches and honor; so much so that there was never another king as rich as he.

But God gave Solomon further instructions. He said, *"And if thou wilt walk in my ways, to keep my statutes and my commandments, as thy father David did walk, then I will lengthen thy days."*

These simple, yet very important instructions are still pertinent in our lives today. How do we follow God's ways and keep His statutes and commandments? It is through our privilege of prayer.

The main point in this passage of scripture is that when we seek God, if we will pray according to His will and His purpose, He will grant us wisdom and discernment to know these things. Because the focus of our prayers is to walk in the will of God, He will then bless us for keeping His commandments, just as He blessed King Solomon.

Spiritual discernment develops over time. God promises to give wisdom if we will just ask for it. However, He doesn't just open our heads and pour it in. It comes from a daily process of seeking His will, studying His word, and listening and obeying the Holy Spirit so that we can better understand. We must be a constant student in the classroom of the Holy Spirit.

Though praying for discernment is very important, much of our obtaining it is through our study of the scriptures. No matter how much we pray, in order to discern God's will, it is necessary for us to see a godly pattern. From beginning to end, the Bible gives us promises and principles to live by. We can obtain wisdom for any situation from His word.

We must also live out what we learn on a continual basis, realizing that sometimes making wrong choices and observing the consequences is the greatest teacher of spiritual discernment.

Have you ever experienced a nagging sense that something is not right? God wants us to know the difference between right and wrong. But what we sometimes fail to realize, is that God also equips His children to choose between what is "good" and what is "best." It is very likely that Satan will reveal something good to us, just before God is going to reveal something great to us. We have all been guilty of jumping at the first and missing the latter.

Those Christians who seek godly discernment, will recognize the Holy Spirit's warning signal to "wait" by the spiritual static that shocks us into the realization that something is not right. The opportunity might look right, but the static will tell us that it is not.

Prayerful, obedient, submissive, and grounded believers will let a good opportunity pass and continue to wait on the best. They will not move forward until the direction is clear from God to do so.

It is in our relationship with our Heavenly Father that we seek and find the spiritual discernment necessary to do His will. He offers it freely. God longs for us to walk in the way that brings Him the greatest glory and in return He blesses us with joy and peace. Our Lord will show us the path to take, but we must be willing and able to judge what is of Him and what is not.

Be careful about where you seek wisdom. Many influential people will try to give you advice. The only reliable measurement for spiritual discernment is God's word.

Meditating in Prayer

Meditation means *lifting our hearts heavenward*. In solitude, we must shift our focus to God and Him alone, drowning out the distractions that may keep us from hearing His voice. Meditation changes our knowledge into experience as the insights we gain in our quiet time with God stay with us to sustain us in our difficult times.

Meditation should begin with a quiet spirit that is *expecting* to hear from God. It is a purposeful act that allows Him the opportunity to respond to our needs and requests.

Why is meditation important in the Christian life?

- *Meditation encourages holiness.*

It is God's desire that we become more like Christ. It is also His desire that we know Him in all His holiness. So why is it that so many people make blind requests to God, not really understanding who He is or His attributes? Why is it that they are eager to make their needs known, but have no desire to deepen their relationship with Him?

In Ephesians 3:14-21, Paul prays for the church of Ephesus. He asks God to strengthen them with the power of the Holy Spirit and for Christ to dwell in their hearts so that they would be grounded in love. Paul addressed these things to a God he knew well – a God *"who is able to do exceeding abundantly above all that we ask or think."*

In actuality, God is able to give us more than we need, more than we ask for, and He is able to accomplish more than we could ever dream. Getting to know Him in His holiness, gives us insight into His unlimited abilities. In quiet submission, (meditation) God is able to speak to us personally.

Because we are confined by a limited knowledge of God, we often assign human traits to Him, not realizing His ability to transcend any earthly problem. Nothing is too big for God to handle, yet many times we resolve to trudge forward in our own strength, rather than giving it to Him. God in His holiness is greater than any person or power in this world. He has the ultimate authority over every living thing. Meditate on His holiness. He can and will create our victories by His power and love.

- *Meditation leads to contentment.*

Spending time alone with God will bring us peace and contentment, even in the midst of trials and struggles. It renews our

39

spirits. Meditation should include time to not only release our anxieties, but to exchange them for God's peace.

- *Meditation can help us realize the needs of others.*

It is one thing to lift up our own needs, but in the process of giving them over to God, we are often reminded of the needs of others. In the process we realize that their needs are greater than our own.

- *Meditation allows us time to rest.*

If we are not careful, we can find our lives in a vicious cycle of activity which can lead to stress, fatigue, and eventually burn-out. This can occur even when the activities are things that are good. We must find time to rest in God.

Jesus encouraged his disciples to get alone in a secluded place and rest a while. Jesus knew then and He knows now, that by resting in Him, our souls can renew and our minds can separate from the fast pace of life, enabling us to draw from His strength.

Resting in God helps us to see what is necessary in our lives and what is not. Psalm 46:10 commands us to *"Be still and know that I am God:"* In other words, God is our number one priority and He is in control of our lives. With this assurance, it is easy to replace striving for resting.

It is so important to set aside time in our schedules to meditate on God's word, to pray for our needs and the needs of others, and to listen, patiently and quietly, for God to answer.

Be careful not to fall into the pitfall of thinking that in order to be holy, you must always be on your knees and alone with God. When this happens, we are of no use to others. The apostle Paul was a servant of Christ who was so devoted to Him that he counted his own life as loss, but he also knew the importance of sharing the gospel with others. Meditation prepares us for usefulness.

Jesus was all about helping others and He wants to be able to "help Himself" to our lives so that He can then use us to help others.

Solving Problems through Prayer

What is the first thing we tend to do when faced with a problem? Yes, you're right. We try to figure out a solution. We might spend a great deal of time trying to patch it up, smooth it over, or cover it up. Sometimes, we might even ask a friend, knowing that what we really want is not an answer, but sympathy.

What we really need is to know that someone loves us and loves God enough to say, "Let's pray about it, together." A person who is walking in the Spirit will direct us to the One who knows all the answers, instead of trying to be the one to give us the answers.

Our ability to solve problems comes from seeking the Lord before a crisis occurs. In times of contentment, we worship Him, read His word, and communicate with Him in prayer. These are godly habits that focus our attention on God, strengthen our faith, and sustain us when the trials do come. Our first response will not be to figure out a solution to our problem.

Instead, the first thing we will do is turn our attention to God, His will, and what He is trying to teach us or how He is trying to work through us. *Many times we try to avoid a problem when, in God's eyes, that problem may be the very thing we need in order to grow to a higher level in our spiritual lives.*

One thing we must realize is that we live in a spiritual "war zone." When we go to our knees to seek God in our problems, we are asking for a battle with Satan. If we want him to see us as devoted prayer warriors, we must make prayer a priority at all times, but especially in times of crisis when we are weak and vulnerable.

As we read in James 1:2-4, our problems result in endurance. *"But let patience have her perfect work, that ye may be perfect and entire, wanting nothing."* This puts our problems and difficulties into perspective. When we realize they are important in our spiritual growth and development, we start to view them as stepping stones; strategically placed along our path to help us grow in our relationship with Christ. That, my friend, is worth any price!

With just the whisper of His name, "Father," we acknowledge our relationship to God, our need for Him, and our desire to be in His presence. Can't you just imagine how much He loves to hear His name uttered from the lips of His children? When we respond to Him in this way, casting all our cares and problems upon Him, we can expect that His response is going to follow.

We all know what it means to have responsibilities; whether it is work, family, school, or church. When our self-sufficiency keeps us from seeking God's will in prayer, we get out of balance and the result is "anxiety."

Though Paul faced his share of trials, he was able to say, *"Be anxious for nothing,"* (Philippians 4:6) because he understood that anxiety reveals a lack of faith. Faith and fear (or worry) cannot live in the same house. Worry drains energy and allows Satan the opportunity

41

to try to divide the mind. Worry is a self-centered approach to dealing with responsibility. Peace, on the other hand, is the consequence of a God-centered approach.

In order to keep our anxiety in check, we must always be ready and willing to present our requests to God, who is ready and totally capable of handling any care we bring to Him. Knowing this, we should learn to go to God first, not as a last resort, because in His presence we will find peace.

The Rewards of Time Well Spent

Communicating with God through prayer is always a benefit and a blessing. The believer who spends time alone with God can expect this reward. King David's psalms often speak of his renewed energy obtained by being alone with God.

While praying, our spirits are quieted and frustration and worry lose their significance. Placing our energy on worshipping God renews our strength and prepares us for battle. Time spent in prayer also revives us emotionally. The sense of God's presence and His love empower us with energy from on high and serve to increase our faith. Time spent in prayer is not a waste of time, it is time well spent.

Many people resist spending time alone with God. Sometimes this is because of a lack of willingness to admit sin. But if we resist God's determination to purify us and conform us to the image of His Son, we weaken our relationship with Him.

A desire to not allow anything to come between us and our Heavenly Father earns us a closer, more intimate relationship with Him and the personal walk with Him that will sustain us through any of life's trials. Communicating with Him through prayer allows us to receive the blessings of being His child. No value can be placed on the lessons learned in His presence.

If we will just devote ourselves to prayer, amazing things will happen in our lives. He will use us as we never dreamed possible and we will discover a relationship with Him that is indescribable.

Ten rewards that accompany a devoted prayer life:
- A growing relationship with Christ.
- A change in perspective: God's way versus our own.
- A positive faith attitude.
- Peace in the midst of our storms.

- A purifying effect on us morally.
- Spiritual growth in every area of our lives.
- A passion to obey God.
- Reliance on God to meet our every need.
- Power in our service for Him.
- Productivity (fruitfulness) in every area of our lives.

Prayer Opens the Door for God to Speak

We can be sure that the words God speaks are always purposeful. Prayer opens the door so that God can communicate. In our communication with God, *His word is the way He most often speaks to us. On the other hand, prayer is the way we speak to Him.*

He wants us to comprehend the truth and we can be sure that we will do this because of the Holy Spirit's presence in us. We are promised that He will guide us into all truth. (John 16:13)

God also wants us to hear Him so that He can conform us into the image of Christ. As we read and study the scriptures, He may use passages we can relate to a particular circumstance we may be going through. Our part is to align and not resist what He is trying to teach us through the power of the Holy Spirit and His written word.

God also wants to communicate to us so that we can communicate to others. Jesus spoke only what the Father had taught Him. We need to be always listening intently for His voice, so that we can be sure of what we are to say when the time comes.

Don't allow yourself to miss what the Lord wants to tell you. Begin now to train yourself to give Him your undivided attention. Allow your disappointments, difficulties, failures, financial crisis, tragedy, and sickness to draw you to Him. Then seek Him in prayer and ask Him to reveal to you what He is trying to say to you through these things.

Take the time to listen, for God still speaks.

When It Seems God Is Not There

During times of spiritual "dryness" we may be spending time in prayer, reading the scriptures, joining in worship, seeking godly counsel, and looking for God around every corner, yet we don't hear Him speak. Is God hiding during these times?

If Christ lives within our hearts and we are led by the indwelling of the Holy Spirit, then why do we sometimes experience these times of dryness?

There is no easy answer to these questions, but here is some insight. Often they occur *when our attention is distracted and we are focusing on anything and everything "but" God.*

Remember this: the Lord does not conceal Himself from His children. Rather, many times we hide ourselves behind our own walls of shame, guilt, or ego. Read Psalm 63 aloud, prayerfully. Ask God for an awareness of His undeniable presence in your life.

Requirements for Answered Prayer

Is there something in your life that you have been praying for repeatedly and maybe for a long time? For instance, it might be a job opportunity, a relationship, a move, or physical healing. God's word gives us *five requirements* for answered prayer. Take the time to evaluate the results of your personal prayer life.

- *To have complete dependence on Christ* as the only grounds on which we can claim blessing. (John 14:13-14) We cannot rely on our own personal merit.
- *To separate ourselves from all known sin.* (Psalm 66:18) For God to answer our prayer midst known sin in our lives, would mean He was condoning our sinfulness.
- *To have faith in God's word.* (Hebrews 11:6) God has conditional and unconditional promises in His word. We must learn which ones are affected by our obedience.
- *To ask in accordance to His will.* (I John 5) Not my will, but Yours, Lord.
- *To be persistent in our request.* (Luke 18:1-8) God is willing to answer our prayers, but He wants us to continue in fervent prayer until He answers with "NO, SLOW, GROW, or GO."

Closing

II Chronicles 7:14 says, *"If my people, which are called by my name, shall humble themselves, and pray and seek my face, and turn from their wicked ways; then will I hear from heaven, and will forgive their sin, and will heal their land."*

If we will do our part, God has promised to forgive us. Not only has He promised to forgive, but also that He would heal our land...our homes...our families...our financial situations and our relationships.

In Proverbs 15:29 we read, *"He hears the prayer of the righteous."* Living "rightly" before God means to walk as Christ; the One who knew the importance of prayer.

The righteous:
- Understand the character of God, based on the scriptures
- Weep for non-believers
- Rejoice and thank God for all things
- Are intent on doing the will of God
- Search for Him with their whole heart

God calls us to live a righteous life. Below are scripture references from the book of Psalms to confirm our responsibility.

1:6 – "For the Lord knoweth the way of the <u>righteous</u>."
5:12 – "for thou Lord, wilt bless the <u>righteous</u>."
34:15 – "The eyes of the Lord are upon the <u>righteous</u>, and his ears are open to their cry."
34:17 – "The <u>righteous</u> cry, and the Lord heareth and delivereth them out of all their trouble."
34:19 – "Many are the afflictions of the <u>righteous</u>: but the Lord delivereth him out of them all."
37:16 – "A little that a <u>righteous</u> man hath is better than the riches of many wicked."
55:22 – "Cast thy burden upon the Lord, and he shall sustain thee: he shall never suffer the <u>righteous</u> to be moved."
64:10 – "The <u>righteous</u> shall be glad in the Lord, and shall trust in him, and all the upright in heart shall glory."

Jeremiah 29:11-13

"For I know the thoughts that I think toward you, saith the Lord, thoughts of peace and not of evil, to give you an expected end. Then shall ye call upon me, and ye shall go and pray unto me, and I will hearken unto you. And ye shall seek me, and find me, when ye shall search for me with all your heart."

God wants only the best for His children. As a child of God, it is so important that we recognize the most valuable privilege God has given us. That privilege is: to be able to come into His presence and commune with Him, through prayer.

God longs for us to fellowship with Him. If we seek Him, we will find Him, if we seek Him with all our heart.

God is glorified in our:
:

Adoration – by giving Him honor and glory for who He is.

Confession – of our sins.

Thanksgiving – for "all" things.

Offer our *Supplications* – with a humble heart that is surrendered to His will and purpose.

We pray:

To – our Heavenly Father – *who reigns*

In – the name of His Son, Jesus – *who intercedes*

By – the power of the Holy Spirit – *who enables*

Example
The "ACTS" of Prayer:

Dear Heavenly Father, I come **to** You **in** the name of Your Son, Jesus Christ, and **by** the power of the Holy Spirit that lives within me.

(Adoration) – I will rejoice and be glad in You, for You are my Rock, my Fortress, my Deliverer, my God, my strength. The heavens declare Your glory. Let my lips sing of your greatness forever.

(Confession) – I acknowledge my sins unto You, deal with me Lord, and teach my Thy ways.

(Thanksgiving) – I thank You, Lord, for Your goodness to me. I sought You and waited patiently for You and You brought me out of a barren land.

46

(Supplication) – You have promised to supply all my needs. I put my trust in You. Show me Thy ways, deliver me, have mercy on me, and create in me a clean heart. I am Thy servant.

(Promise) – I know You have heard my plea and I know You have received my prayer, because I seek You with all my heart."

In the name of Your precious Son I pray. Amen.

(My personal testimony)
God Answered My Prayer

I asked God for strength that I might achieve.
I was made weak that I might learn humbly to obey.
I asked God for health that I might do greater things.
I was given infirmity that I might do better things.
I asked for riches that I might be happy.
I was given poverty that I might be wise.
I asked for power that I might have the praise of men.
I was given weakness that I might feel the need for God.
I asked for all things that I might enjoy life.
I was given life that I might enjoy all things.
I got nothing that I asked for – but everything I needed and hoped for.
My prayers were answered
I am richly blessed.(Author Unknown)

I pray that today will be a day of new beginnings and greater understanding. May the God of all wisdom and might draw each of us closer and closer to His heart as we "Ask, Seek, and Knock." It is then that He will pour into our lives all manner of blessings; more abundantly than we could ever imagine. He loves us this much!

The most important prayer we will ever pray is one of repentance and acceptance of Jesus Christ as our personal Savior. The prayer of confession of sins and acceptance is the only prayer that God responds to when it comes to the non-believer.

Have you taken the time to pray and ask Christ to be Lord of your life? It's a simple prayer, but first I want you to ask yourself these questions:

1. Do you believe that you are a sinner and that Christ died for your sins, was buried, and rose again?
2. Do you want forgiveness for your sins and God's promise of eternal life in Heaven?
3. Are you ready to open the door of your heart, to ask Jesus to come in, and then to surrender your life to Him? If so, then pray this prayer:

Heavenly Father, I realize that I am a sinner. I ask you to forgive me of my sins. I believe that You sent Your Son, Jesus Christ, to die on a cross for my sins and that He rose again to give me eternal life. I now ask Jesus to come into my heart and become Lord of my life. This I ask of You, Father, in the name of Jesus Christ I pray, Amen.

In order to help you put into practice the "ACTS" of prayer, I have included a compilation of some of my favorite verses from the book of Psalms. Each day, choose a verse from: Adoration, Confession, Thanksgiving, and Supplication (in this order) until you have created a consistent, continual, fervent and effective habit of prayer.
You will be blessed.
May the God of all grace bless you as you put the wisdom you have gained into "action."
Karen

The "ACTS" of Praying through the Psalms

Adoration

3:3 – "But thou, O Lord, art a shield for me; my glory, and the lifter up of mine head."

5:3 – "in the morning will I direct my prayer unto thee, and will look up."

5:11 "But let all those that put their trust in thee rejoice."

7:17 – "I will praise the Lord according to his righteousness: and will sing praise to the name of
the Lord most high."

9:2 – "I will be glad and rejoice in thee."

10:16 – "The Lord is King for ever and ever."

18:2 – "The Lord is my rock, and my fortress, and my deliverer; my God, my strength, in whom I will trust."

19:1 – "The heavens declare the glory of God; and the firmament showeth his handiwork."

21:13 – "Be thou exalted, Lord, in thine own strength: so will we sing and praise thy power."

27:1 – "The Lord is my light ad my salvation; whom shall I fear? The Lord is the strength
of my life; of whom shall I be afraid?"

28:7 – "The Lord is my strength and my shield; my heart trusted in him, and I am helped; therefore my heart greatly rejoiceth; and with my song will I praise him."

29:2 – "Give unto the Lord the glory due unto his name; worship the Lord in the beauty of holiness."

Psalm 30: 1-12 – "I will extol (glorify, celebrate highly, praise) thee, O Lord; for thou hast lifted me up,
O Lord, I cried unto thee, and thou hast healed me."
O Lord, thou hast brought up my soul from the grave; thou hast kept me alive,
Weeping may endure for a night, but joy cometh in the morning.
I shall never be moved.
Lord, by thy favour thou hast made my mountain to stand strong;
I cried unto thee, O Lord, and unto the Lord I made supplication.
Hear, O Lord, and have mercy upon me: Lord, be thou my helper.
Thou hast turned for me my mourning into dancing: thou hast put off my sackcloth, and girded me with gladness;

To the end that my glory my sing praise to thee, and not be silent, O Lord my God, I will give thanks unto thee for ever."
34:1 – "I will bless the Lord at all times: his praise shall continually be in my mouth."
34:3 – "O magnify the Lord with me, and let us exalt his name together."
35:18 – "I will give thee thanks in the great congregation: I will praise thee among much people."
35:27 – "Let the Lord be magnified."
35:28 – "And my tongue shall speak of thy righteousness and of thy praise all the day long."
46:1 – "God is our refuge and strength, a very present help in trouble."
47:1 – "shout unto God with the voice of trumph."
48:1 – "Great is the Lord, and greatly to be praised."
51:15 – "O Lord, upon thou my lips: and my mouth shall show forth thy praise."
57:9 – "I will praise thee, O Lord, among the people: I will sing unto thee among the nations."
57:11 – "Be thou exalted, O God, above the heavens: let thy glory be above all the earth."
63:4-7 – "I will bless thee while I live: I will lift up my hands in thy name." My mouth shall praise thee with joyful lips; in the shadow of thy wings will I rejoice."
71:8 – "Let my mouth be filled with thy praise and with thy honour all the day."
71:23 – "My lips shall greatly rejoice when I sing unto thee. My tongue also shall talk of thy righteousness all the day long."
73:25 – "Whom have I in heaven but thee? and there is none upon earth that I desire beside thee."
79:13 – "So we thy people, and sheep of thy pasture will give thee thanks for ever: we will show forth thy praise to all generations."
89:1 – "with my mouth will I make known thy faithfulness to all generations."
96:4,6,8,9 – "For the Lord is great, and greatly to be praised:" Honor and majesty are before him, strength and beauty are in his sanctuary. Give unto the Lord the glory due unto his name: O worship the Lord in the beauty of holiness: fear before him, all the earth."
98:4 – "Make a joyful noise unto the Lord, all the earth:"
103:1-6,8,17 – "Bless the Lord, O my soul; and all that is within me, bless his holy name.

Bless the Lord, O my soul, and forget not all his benefits:
Who forgiveth all thine iniquities; who healeth all thy diseases;
Who redeemeth thy life from destruction; who crowneth thee with
loving kindness and tender mercies.
Who satisfieth thy mouth with good things; so that thy youth is
renewed like the eagle's.
The Lord executeth rigthteousness and judgment for all that are
oppressed.
The Lord is merciful an gracious, slow to anger, and plenteous in
mercy.
But the mercy of the Lord is from everlasting to everlasting upon them
that fear him,"
104:31 – "The glory of the Lord shall endure for ever."
115:1 – "Not unto us, O Lord, not unto us, but unto thy name give
glory,"
118:24 – "This is the day which the Lord hath made; we will rejoice
and be glad in it."
118:28 – "Thou art my God, and I will praise thee: thou art my God
and I will exalt thee."
119:171,173,175 – "My lips shall utter praise, when thou hast taught
me thy statutes. Let thine hand help me; for I have chosen thy
precepts. Let my soul live, and it shall praise thee;"
139:14 – "I will praise thee; for I am fearfully and wonderfully
made."
149:5 – Let the saints be joyful in glory: let them sing aloud upon their
beds."
150: 1-6 – "Praise ye the Lord. Praise Gods in his sanctuary: praise
him in the firmament of his power. Praise him for his mighty acts;
praise him according to his excellent greatness. Praise him with the
sound of the trumpet: praise him with the psaltery and harp. Praise
him with the timbrel and dance: praise him with stringed instruments
and organs. Praise him upon the loud cymbals: praise him upon the
high sounding cymbals. Let everything that hath breath praise the
Lord. Praise ye the Lord."

Confession

7:8 – "Judge me, O Lord, according to my righteousness, and
according to mine integrity that is in me."

19:12-13 – "Who can understand his errors? Cleanse thou me from secret faults. Keep back thy servant also from presumptuous sins; let them not have dominion over me:"

22:22 – "I will declare thy name unto my brethren; in the midst of the congregation will I praise thee."

22:25 – "My praise shall be of thee in the great congregation."

24:10 – "the Lord of hosts, he is the King of glory."

25:7 – "Remember not the sins of my youth, nor my transgressions: according to thy mercy."

25:18 – "Look upon mine affliction and my pain; and forgive all my sins."

26:1 – "Judge me, O Lord, for I have walked in mine integrity:" Examine me, O Lord, and prove me; try my reins and my heart."

27:8 – "When thou saidest, Seek ye my face; my heart said unto thee, Thy face, Lord, will I seek."

31:5 – "Unto thy hand I commit my spirit."

31:15 – "My times are in thy hands."

32:5 – "I acknowledged my sin unto thee, and mine iniquity gave I not hid. I said, I will confess my transgressions unto the Lord; and thou forgavest the iniquity of my sin."

39:8 – "Deliver me from all my transgressions."

51:17 – "The sacrifices of God are a broken spirit: a broken and contrite heart,"

66:18 – "If I regard iniquity in my heart, the Lord will not hear me."

73:28 – "But it is good for me to draw nigh to God; I have put my trust in the Lord God."

77:1-6 - "I cried unto God with my voice, and he gave ear unto me. In the day of my trouble I sought the Lord: my soul ceased to be comforted.

I remembered God, and was troubled: I complained and my spirit was overwhelmed.

Thou holdest mie eyes waking: I am so troubled that I cannot speak.

I call to remembrance my song in the night. I commune with mine own heart."

107:2 – "Let the redeemed of the Lord say so,"

107:8-9 – "Oh that men would praise the Lord for his goodness, and for his wonderful works to the children of men! For he satisfieth the longing soul, and filleth the hungry soul with goodness."

118:17-19 – "I shall not die, but live, and declare the works of the Lord. The Lord has chastened me sore: but he hath not given me over

unto death. Open to me the gates of righteousness: I will go into them, and I will praise the Lord."
119:124 – "Deal with thy servant according unto thy mercy, and teach me thy statutes."
119:176 – "I have gone astray like a lost sheep; seek thy servant; for I do not forget thy commandments."
143:10 – "Teach me to do thy will; for thou art my God:"

Thanksgiving

3:5 – "I laid me down and slept; I awaked; for the Lord sustained me."
4:8 – "I will both lay me down in peace and sleep; for thou, Lord, only makest me dwell in safety."
9:13 – "Have mercy upon me, O Lord, thou that hast liftest me up from the gates of death."
13:5 – "I have trusted in thy mercy; my heart shall rejoice in thy salvation. I will sing unto the Lord because he hath dealt bountifully with me."
18:19 – "He brought me forth also into a large place; he delivered me, because he delighted in me."
18:20 – "The Lord rewarded me according to my righteousness."
18:21 – "For I have kept the ways of the Lord, and have not wickedly departed from my God."
19:7-11 – "The law of the Lord is perfect, converting the soul; the testimony of the Lord is sure, making wise the simple. The statues of the Lord are right, rejoicing the heart: the commandments of the Lord is pure, enlightening the eyes. The fear of the Lord is clean, enduring for ever: the judgments of the Lord are true and righteous altogether. More to be desired are they than gold, yea, than much fine gold: sweeter also than honey and the honeycomb. Moreover by them is thy servant warned: an in keeping of them there is great reward."
27:5 – "For in the time of trouble he shall hide me in his pavilion: he shall set me upon a rock."
27:13 – "I had fainted, unless I had believed to see the goodness of the Lord in the land of the living."
31:4 – "give thanks at the remembrance of his holiness."
31:7 – "I will be glad and rejoice in thy mercy: for thou hast considered my trouble; thou hast known my soul in adversities."
32:7 – "Thou art my hiding place; thou shalt preserve me from trouble; thou shalt compass me about with songs of deliverance.'

34:4 – "I sought the Lord, and he heard me, and delivered me from all my fears."
40:1-3 – "I waited patiently for the Lord; and he inclined unto me, and heard my cry.
He brought me up also out of an horrible pit, out of the miry clay, and set my feet upon a rock, and established my goings.
And he hath put a new song in my mouth, even praise unto our God: many shall see it, ad fear, and shall trust in the Lord."
40:5 – "Many, O Lord my God, are thy wonderful works which thou hast done, and thy thoughts which are to usward. I would declare and speak of them, they are more than can be numbered."
40:8 – "I delight to do thy will, O my God, yea, thy law is within my heart."
63:1 – "O God, thou art my God; early will I seek thee: my soul thirsteth for thee, my flesh longeth for thee in a dry and thirsty land,"
65:4 – "Blessed is the man whom thou choosest, and causeth to approach unto thee,"
69:30 – "I will praise the name of God with a song, and will magnify him with thanksgiving."
71:17 – "O God, thou hast taught me from my youth: and hitherto have I declared thy wondrous works."
92:4 – "For thou, Lord, hast made me glad through thy work: I will triumph in the works of thy hands."
94:17,19 – "Unless the Lord had been my help, my soul had almost dwelt in silence. In the multitude of my thoughts within me thy comforts delight my soul."
95:2 – "Let us come before his presence with thanksgiving, and make a joyful noise unto him with psalms."
119:71,73,75,77,93, – "It is good for me that I have been afflicted; that I might learn thy statutes. Thy hands have made me and fashioned me: give me understanding, that I may learn thy commandments. I know, O Lord, that thy judgments are right, and that thou in faithfulness hast afflicted me. Let thy tender mercies come unto me, that I may live: for thy law is my delight. I will never forget thy precepts: for with them thou hast quickened me,"
119:105 – "Thy word is a lamp unto my feet, and a light unto my path."
120:1 – "In my distress I cried unto the Lord, and he heard me."
121:1-2 – "I will lift up mine eyes unto the hills, from whence cometh my help. My help cometh from the Lord, which made heaven and

earth. He will not suffer thy foot to be moved; he that keepeth thee will not slumber."

142:3 – "When my spirit was overwhelmed within me, then thou knewest my path."

Supplication

5:8 – "Lead me, O Lord, in thy righteousness; make my way straight before my face."

6:2 – "Have mercy upon me, O Lord, for I am weak; O Lord, heal me;"

7:1 – "O Lord, my God, in thee do I put my trust: save me from all them that persecute me, and deliver me."

17:5 – "Hold up my goings in thy paths, that my footsteps slip not."

17:8 – "Keep me as the apple of the eye, hide me under the shadow of thy wings."

19:14 – "Let the words of my mouth, and the meditation of my heart, be acceptable in thy sight, O Lord, my strength, and my redeemer."

25:4 – "Show me thy ways, O Lord, teach me thy paths."

25:5 – "Lead me in thy truth, and teach me: for thou art the God of my salvation; on thee do I wait all the day."

25:16-17 – Turn thee unto me, and have mercy upon me; for I am desolate and afflicted." The troubles of my heart are enlarged: O bring thou me out of my distresses."

25:20 – "O keep my soul, and deliver me: let me not be ashamed; for I put my trust in thee."

26:21 – "Let integrity and uprightness preserve me; for I wait on thee.'

27:4 – "One thing have I desired of the Lord, that will I seek after; that I may dwell in the house of the Lord all the days of my life, to behold the beauty of the Lord,"

27:7 – "Hear, O Lord, when I cry with my voice: have mercy also upon me, and answer me."

27:9 – "Hide not thy face far from me; put not thy servant away in anger: thou hast been my help; leave me not, neither forsake me, O God of my salvation."

27:11 – "Teach me thy way, O Lord, and lead me in a plain path."

28:2 – "Hear the voice of my supplications, when I cry unto thee,"

31:3 – "For thy name's sake lead me, and guide me."

31:16 – "Make thy face to shine upon thy servant."

39:12 – Hear my prayer, O Lord, and give ear unto my cry;"

39:13 – "O spare me, that I may recover strength, before I go hence, and be no more."

51:10-13 – "Create in me a clean heart, O God, and renew a right spirit within me. Cast me not away from thy presence; and take not thy holy spirit from me. Restore unto me the joy of thy salvation; and uphold me with thy free spirit. Then will I teach transgressors thy ways, and sinners shall be converted unto thee."

61:1-2 – "Hear my cry, O God; attend unto my prayer. When my heart is overwhelmed; lead me to the rock that is higher than I."

102:2 – "Hide not thy face from me in the day when I am in trouble; incline thine ear unto me: in the day when I call answer me speedily."

119:65 – "Thou hast dealt well with thy servant, O Lord, according unto thy word. Teach me good judgment and knowledge: for I have believed thy commandments. Before I was afflicted I went astray: but now have I kept thy word. Teach me thy statutes.

119:133 – "Order my steps."

138:8 – "thy mercy, O Lord, endureth for ever; forsake not the works of thine own hands."

"Precious Promises" to include in your "ACTS" of Prayer

1:3 – "And he shall be like a tree planted by the rivers of water, that bringeth forth his fruit in his season; his leaf also shall not wither; and whatsoever he doeth shall prosper."

6:9 – "The Lord hath heard my supplication; the Lord will receive my prayer."

9:9 – "The Lord also will be a refuge for the oppressed, a refuge in times of trouble. And they that know thy name will put their trust in thee: for thou, Lord, hast not forsaken them that seek thee."

16:11 – "Thou wilt show me the path of life: in thy presence is fullness of joy; at thy right hand there are pleasures for evermore."

27:10 – "When my father and my mother forsake me, then the Lord will take me up."

27:14 – "Wait on the Lord: be of good courage, and he shall strengthen thine heart: wait I say, on the Lord."

29:11 – "The Lord will give strength unto his people; the Lord will bless his people with peace."

31:23-24 – "O love the Lord, al ye his saints, for the Lord preserveth the faithful, and plentifully rewardeth the proud doer." Be of good courage, and he shall strengthen your heart, all ye that hope in the Lord."

33:4 – "For the word of the Lord is right; and all his works are done in truth."

34:7 – "The angel of the Lord encampeth round about them that fear him, and delivereth them."

34:10 – "They that seek the Lord shall not want any good thing."

37:4 – "Delight thyself also in the Lord; and he shall give thee the desires of thine heart."

37:7 – "Rest in the Lord, and wait patiently for him."

  9 – "those that wait upon the Lord, they shall inherit the earth."

  34 – "Wait on the Lord, and keep his way, and he shall exalt thee to inherit the land."

37:23 – The steps of a good man are ordered by the Lord: and he delighteth in his way."

46:10 – "Be still, and know that I am God."

51:22 – "Cast thy burden upon the Lord, and he shall sustain thee: he shall never suffer the righteous to be moved."

68:6 – "he bringeth out those which are bound with chains."

91:11 – "For he shall give his angels charge over thee, to keep thee in all thy ways."

103:12 – "As far as the east is from the west, so fare hath he removed our transgressions from us."

107:29 – "He maketh the storm a calm, so that the waves there of are still."

118:9 – "It is better to trust in the Lord than to put confidence in man."

126:5 – "They that sow in tears shall reap in joy. He that goeth forth and weepeth, bearing precious seed, shall doubtless come again with rejoicing, bringing his sheaves with him."

138:8 – "The Lord will perfect that which concerneth me:"

145:14 – "The Lord upholdeth all that fall, and raiseth up all those that be bowed down."

145:19-20 – "He will fulfil the desire of them that fear him: he also will hear their cry, and will save them. The Lord preserveth all them that love him."

Review

_____ is the most important, yet most neglected activity in the Christian life.

Prayer is essential if we want to have a _____ with God.

In Matthew 6, the disciples made the request of Jesus, _____.

A - _____
C - _____
T - _____
I - _____
O - _____
N - _____
S - _____

What the Lord really wants to give us through prayer is _____.

_____ is considered to be our "model prayer."

P - _____
R - _____
A - _____
Y - _____
E - _____
R - _____

A - _____
C - _____
T - _____
S - _____

A -

_____

_____

C -

_____

_____

T -

_____

_____

S -

_____

_____

The price of prayerlessness is

_____

Three things we must do in order to pray "in the name of Jesus:"

_____

_____

_____

_____ and it shall be given you
_____ and ye shall find
_____ and it shall be opened unto you

Hindrances to our prayers:

_____

_____

_____

_____

_____

_____

_____

_____

_____

_____

The power in our prayer life is in _____.

A prayer-less person is a _____ person.

_____ is receiving what we do not deserve.
_____ is God's way of preventing us from receiving what we do deserve.

Waiting on God is a _____, _____, _____, _____, anticipation of what God is going to do in our lives.

Reasons why we should always wait on God:

_____
_____
_____
_____

What happens when we fail to wait?

_____
_____

If our request is out of His will, God says, _____.
If it is not in His time, God says, _____.
If our motive is wrong, God says, _____.
If our request, timing, and motive is right, God says, _____!

In order for us to wait we will need:

_____
_____
_____
_____
_____
_____
_____
_____
_____

It is the _____who teaches us how to pray.

Meditation means to _____.

Our ability to solve problems comes from seeking the Lord,

_____.

Ten rewards for a devoted prayer life:

_____
_____
_____
_____

_____

_____

_____

_____

_____

_____

In our communication with God, _____ is most often the way
He speaks to us, but _____ is the way we speak to Him.

If we are experiencing spiritual "dryness," it is likely our
_____ is distracted and our _____ is on anything,
but God.

Five requirements for answered prayer:

_____

_____

_____

_____

_____

For book ordering information or to schedule a speaking engagement, please contact:

Karen Faith McGowan
Faith to Finish Ministry
PO Box 204534
Augusta, Georgia 30917
706-449-2863
or
website: FaithtoFinish.com / email: Karen@FaithtoFinish.com

Karen is also the author of *"Faith to Finish."* This book contains a personal story about how her faith sustained her and gave her hope and deliverance through the most difficult time in her life. Karen very candidly shares the experience of what she calls, "A Close Encounter of Three Kinds." She says that it was her faith that kept her running in the race. (as described in Hebrews 12:1-2) You will be encouraged to read how God used the experience to draw her closer to Himself and thereby, changed her life forever.

"Finding Faith to Finish" was written to be used as a handbook for those whose desire is to develop or deepen their relationship with God. It is based on several different aspects of Karen's life that she feels have had significant impact on her walk with God and resulting spiritual growth. However, she is quick to admit that she is still a work in progress.

While she was in a coma, she says, "God gave me specific instructions for the next portion of my life's race." In order to fulfill her commitment, she not only has written three books, but she shares her testimony, wherever God leads. It is her goal to inspire others to keep running in their race, knowing that all things in life happen for a reason, when we love God and when we are called according to His purpose.

The handbook can be used for personal or group Bible study. These two books are not sold separately. They can be ordered using the contact information listed above.

Karen is available to share her inspiring testimony in word and in song.